PRAISE FOR BILLY-RAY BELCOURT /
NDN COPING MECHANISMS

Winner, Stephan G. Stephansson Award for Poe
Finalist, Robert Kroetsch City of Edmonton Book Prize
Finalist, Lambda Literary Award for Gay Poetry
Finalist, Raymond Souster Award
Longlist, CBC Canada Reads
A *Library Journal* Best Book of the Year
A CBC Book of the Year

"Both intellectual and visceral, these poems dazzle with metaphoric richness and striking lyricism." — *Toronto Star*

"An impressive follow-up to his first book." — *Winnipeg Free Press*

"For all the ferocious energy and one-two punch of language here, this is also a concentrated, beautifully managed work." — *Library Journal*, STARRED REVIEW

"A masterful blend of the personal and the political, the ephemeral and the corporeal, the theoretical and the emotional." — *Quill & Quire*

"[Billy-Ray Belcourt's] words shake with their own power." — *Adroit Journal*

"Playful, candid, and campy." — *Prairie Books NOW*

"NDN *Coping Mechanisms* is a haunting book that dreams a new world — a 'holy place filled with NDN girls, hair wet with utopia' — as it simultaneously excoriates the world that 'is a wound' and the historic and present modalities of violence against Indigenous peoples under Canadian settler colonialism. Belcourt considers the genocidal nation-state, queerness, and the limits and potential of representation, often through a poetic/scholarly lineage that includes Leanne Betasamosake Simpson, Saidiya Hartman, Anne Boyer, José Esteban Muñoz, Christina Sharpe, and Gwen Benaway, among others. This is the beautiful achievement of NDN *Coping Mechanisms*: Belcourt conjures a sovereign literary space that refuses white sovereignty and is always already in relation to the ideas of the foremost decolonial poets and thinkers of Turtle Island."
— Mercedes Eng, author of *Prison Industrial Complex Explodes*

"This brilliant book is endlessly giving, lingering in tight spaces within the forms of loneliness, showing us their contours. These poems do the necessary work of negotiating with the heart-killing present from which we imagine and make Indigenous futures. Every line feels like a possible way out of despair." — Elissa Washuta, author of *My Body Is a Book of Rules*

"'I believe I exist. / To live, one can be neither / more nor less hungry than that.' How grateful I am that Billy-Ray Belcourt and these poems believe in themselves enough to exist. With prodigious clarity, this work moves swiftly amongst theory and prose, longing and lyric, questioning and coping, 'not dying' and 'obsessively apologizing to the moon for all that she has to witness.' It is not hyperbole to say these poems are brilliant. And so brilliantly, searingly, they live."
— TC Tolbert, author of *Gephyromania*

NDN COPING MECHANISMS

ALSO BY BILLY-RAY BELCOURT

This Wound is a World

A History of My Brief Body

NDN COPING MECHANISMS

NOTES FROM THE FIELD

BILLY-RAY BELCOURT

ANANSI

Published in Canada in 2019 and the USA in 2019 by House of Anansi Press Inc.
www.houseofanansi.com

House of Anansi Press is committed to protecting our natural environment. This book is made of material from well-managed FSC®-certified forests, recycled materials, and other controlled sources.

House of Anansi Press is a Global Certified Accessible™ (GCA by Benetech) publisher. The ebook version of this book meets stringent accessibility standards and is available to readers with print disabilities.

26 25 24 23 22   6 7 8 9 10

Library and Archives Canada Cataloguing in Publication

Title: NDN coping mechanisms : notes from the field / Billy-Ray Belcourt
Other titles: Indian coping mechanisms
Names: Belcourt, Billy-Ray, author.
Description: Poems.
Identifiers: Canadiana (print) 20190043369 | Canadiana (ebook) 20190043385 | ISBN 9781487005771 (softcover) | ISBN 9781487005795 (hardcover) | ISBN 9781487005788 (EPUB) | ISBN 9781487007164 (Kindle)
Classification: LCC PS8603.E516 N46 2019 | DDC C811/.6—dc23

Library of Congress Control Number: 2019930411

Cover image: Meryl McMaster
Cover design: Alysia Shewchuk
Text design and typesetting: Laura Brady

House of Anansi Press respectfully acknowledges that the land on which we operate is the Traditional Territory of many Nations, including the Anishinabeg, the Wendat, and the Haudenosaunee. It is also the Treaty Lands of the Mississaugas of the Credit.

 Canada Council Conseil des Arts
for the Arts du Canada

 ONTARIO ARTS COUNCIL
CONSEIL DES ARTS DE L'ONTARIO
an Ontario government agency
un organisme du gouvernement de l'Ontario

We acknowledge for their financial support of our publishing program the Canada Council for the Arts, the Ontario Arts Council, and the Government of Canada.

Printed and bound in Canada

 MIX
Paper from
responsible sources
FSC
www.fsc.org FSC® C103567

For those who have survived history and those who haven't.

. . . I wasn't trying to make a sentence — I was trying to break free. — Ocean Vuong

Words bounce. — Anne Carson

CONTENTS

NDN is internet shorthand used by Indigenous peoples in North America to refer to ourselves. It is also sometimes an acronym meaning "Not Dead Native."

I.

A COUNTRY IS HOW MEN HUNT

What constitutes an NDN? A myth
doused in midnight? A soul
in the shape of a clenched fist?
Concerning the collapse of organized human life,
I demand my two cents be taken seriously:
God sends his pale horsemen westward every fucking day!
Canadian history — or, how to wage war
on an emotion. For a century,
no one spoke of the extinction of joy.
A village emptied of its children is a haunting.
Every natural phenomenon becomes an elegiac gesture.
Am I a war hero
if I succumb to Mother Nature's fury
and not to my captor's?
Poets pledge allegiance to a country I don't believe in.
A country is how men hunt in the dark.
A man I love but don't trust kisses me
the way a soldier might press his face into the soil of his old country.
I am a Museum of Modern Misery he storms through.
Which is to say the body signals a crisis of representation.
The body is an archive when it heralds an indictment.
My suffering will multiply.
So what if in the end my living amounts to an evidentiary act.

What I wanted was what I asked for.

I saw my kokum for the first time in weeks.

Miraculously, she is still alive.

All morning I picked bits and pieces of history from her hair.

NDN BROTHERS

Loneliness finds me drunk
in an old Billy-Ray Belcourt poem.
What's important is that wherever I am
my brother is perched on my right cheekbone.

We are twenty-four and already too old
for our own good. Last night felt like our last night.
They always do. This is what makes night nightly
in an amnestic nation against the literature of treason.

Behind the wheel of a car without headlights,
the night is a lukewarm mouth we sing into.
In other words, where the heterogeneity of grief
meets the singularity of death is the NDN experience.

Today, the Ministry of Historical Ignorance
didn't keep me and my brother safe.
With its extralegal powers, the Ministry brought us to our knees
so as to clog our throats with polluted language.

In defiance, we licked the walls dirty
in a house of administered subjectivity.
Don't blame us. Our last hope: a fever
is sunlight breaking apart inside the skull.

THE TERRIBLE BEAUTY OF THE RESERVE

after Saidiya Hartman

Everyone's uncle thinks he is the world's
most handsome NDN and no one says otherwise.

Rez dogs roam about without having to perform
emotional labour for humans. They eat

where they are welcomed, which is everywhere.
Most who live here don't know they are in the ruins

of a failed experiment of epic proportions. Teens blaze
to feel the euphoria of being outside memory.

We all bathe in the sociality of the hangover.
It isn't that no one has time for themselves, it is that they are

always playing cards or talking about Connor McDavid
or carpooling to bingo or babysitting their brothers' kids.

We all owe something to someone, so we congregate
under the presumption of debt and this is always-already.

We all joke about falling in love with our cousins,
but we are all perpetually falling in love with our cousins

in a platonic way, because we grew up together and
no one was alienated by the tyranny of the couple form.

Vehicles pass through in droves, but no one looks, so we disappear,
hands intertwined, into the freedom of a shimmering anonymity.

A LOVER'S DISCOURSE

A boy in love with a boy
                becomes an open window.
In every account of my adolescence,
                    I hurled myself at a prison
so that moonlight could tiptoe inside
                        — the captive jutted out of me like music!
Explanation: homos, like poems,
                like city streets, are self-degrading.
(The sex drive and the death drive
                are one and the same.)
In the forest of men, shame dripped
                from my mouth, a kind of honey.
When I was licked clean and left
                with nothing, I made
something lifelike in a kingdom
                with my cursed brethren.
My lover traded in his horns
                for citizenship.
We were grateful to be more
                than a cliff-bound herd of buffalo.
Alas, we couldn't drink
                from the same river twice,

but we kept at it, knee-deep in saliva.

        In our dying days,

I stood on his shoulders

        to tug at low-level rainclouds.

With a butter knife,

        I sculpted us a paranoid's paradise.

A discovery:

        even God's roof is bullet-holed!

WHAT TO AN NDN IS THE INTRINSIC GOODNESS OF MANKIND?

I bottle up my feelings. In my serrated hands,
the bottle shatters and still I am not free.
What is freedom to a man
with shards of glass moving through him?
I want to write as though the sentence were a set of limbs
to be puppeteered.
With which words will I undertake this work of choreography?
I dabbled in documentary poetics,
but my sexual practices made me anti-systemological.
I filmed every inconsequential second of my queer life
and called it Experimental Cinema.
When no one was looking,
I invented post-structuralism.
Who but an NDN would know that some days truth is a ghost
who shouts in the voice of no one in particular and other days
it is a secret nostalgia poured into the coffee cups of the living?
Apropos of everything, what to an NDN
is the intrinsic goodness of mankind?
Maybe justice *is* a lover who regurgitates the English language
so it comes back sweeter.
Canada, why are your elevators filled with mud water?
What is it about a palm

that makes a country feel like a garden?
I dug and dug.
I pulled out a bouquet of skyscrapers.
I kissed each window softly.
Is this not what an NDN does in a poem?

THE WALL CLOCK CAUGHT FIRE FROM NEGLECT

Yes, this is the bedroom
      I built to evoke the effect
of an open-air church.
        Just once, I wanted
to be unhinged from sentimentality.
        Instead, I continue to aim
my tongue at a mattress
        covered in moss soft as September.
Which each bite I mutter:
        What an ugly, necessary monster I made of myself.
I think it is midnight
        — the wall clock caught fire
from neglect a long time ago.
        My grief crowbarred the door open.
It is like a coffin:
        inviting a gaze in response
to which it can't spit back a body.
        The landlord fastens a note
to my forehead: HALF-EXISTENCE
        IS STRUCTURALLY AKIN TO AN APARTMENT.
He lays himself flat in the hallway,
        like a welcome mat.

A creature of habit, I dip my feet
           into the dirt of yet another man's chest.
His exhales gunfire.
           I float to the ceiling, light
scurrying from me like water
           in search of a resting place.
I miss Billy-Ray Belcourt.
           I believed myself
capable of holding on to a name.
           I was wrong. A man
called me beautiful tonight,
           so I started over once more
— the old body still flickering beside me.
           Tomorrow, I will watch a boy
who looks like me
           walk into oncoming traffic.
He will expect no one to stop,
           but everyone will.
People love being alive so much
           they will force aliveness
onto even a hypothesis of a man.
           I am a man,
but only insofar as I spontaneously combust
           when the best possible world begins.
So, each night I make love
           the way one siphons gasoline

from an abandoned car:
    as though I am running out of time.
Truth is, I want even less
    than this already puny life.

I BECOME LESS OF WHO I AM BY THE SECOND

Boy becomes a 3-D printing of a man.
It is comforting to think of my gender as a farmer's field
already rototilled, already tidied up.
I become less of who I am by the second.
Look at the branches growing from my teeth!
Then there's the doe, tipsy on me,
grazing to no end.
Were I to speak, I'd look
like a cracked windshield.
My two hundred and six lonely bones
have each acquired a type of consciousness.
They pretend not to harbour bad feelings about me,
my ungodly molecularity.
What can I say about my shadow?
It loves the unlit street
more than it does me.
Sometimes a body is that which happens to you.
Every day, dime-sized holes germinate on my flesh,
as though I were trying to free myself from myself.
I will go on like this forever:
the earth ringing in my chest.

CREE GIRL BLOWS UP THE NECROPOLIS OF OTTAWA

In the first seven minutes of Jeff Barnaby's *Rhymes for Young Ghouls*, Anna (Roseanne Supernault) kills herself, and who but her daughter Aila (Devery Jacobs) is left to witness her body suspended in thick air. "The day I found my mother dead, I aged a thousand years," she says from the future. Aila goes on to take the helm of a drug-dealing business and to seek revenge against the Indian agent who with vicious precision erodes the social worlds of those living on the reserve. If I were to make a short film, it would be about a Cree girl who builds a time machine fuelled by the feeling power of grieving kokums. She would obliterate herself and be born anew in a time in which one could be a Cree girl and desire a world outside the field of vision of what are now two ministries of NDN misery. In fact, the opening sequence would be shot via a hand-held camera as the Cree girl blows up the necropolis of Ottawa. NDN possibility would flower everywhere outside the frame. That is, the film wouldn't be about the bloodied hands of history or what it is to be but an object of sorrow in the eyes of the reconciler and the executioner alike. Instead, we would see the Cree girl solely through a low-angle shot and at no point would she be anything but a cartographer who charts a world in her own image and no one else's.

Joussard, AB

AT THE MERCY OF THE SKY

In front of me:
1947, a fractured door,
rotted wooden beams.
Behind:
an ancient forest of gone peoples.
This is what's left of a residential school in Joussard, Alberta.
What remains exceeds the infrastructural remains.
We are mired in the afterlife of captivity.
Cages were made out of bodies,
and then bodies out of anything left behind.
This is the world we have inherited.
It is infused with the violence of being forced to float
in the air like an unanswered question.
It is an afternoon in June when I return to this primal
scene, this open wound.
The air clots, as if to make a fool out of my lungs,
to remind me that having a body is a sick
fucking joke I was never in on.
Air enters, and out comes smoke.
There is something unsayable about this type of return.
It makes words crumble in my mouth.

They taste like dirt this time.
It feels NDN to be pulled into a scene of objection like this one.
It is summer, so rich white people
are camped on the shores of Lesser Slave Lake,
just a few feet away from this prison house.
They think nothing of it.
Not thinking is a way to think the world.
They are submerged in an aroma of violence only the hunted can detect,
but unlike mine, their sense of self remains intact.
A self that's been dragged through the mud
of bad social structures can't bear this kind of looking.
One day, the Government of Alberta
might make this place into a historic site.
I can see it now:
a spectacle during which white politicians crawl
out of the bloody maw of the past,
smiling with the carcasses of words
like "history" and "empathy" hanging from their lips.
They pretend the red on their skin is sunlight.
To be NDN is to know a spectacle isn't always an event.
I am fixed by the darkness that emanates from the doorway.
It is a thick nothingness at which I feel compelled to stare.
Nothingness is a world unto itself.
A lot of NDNs live there.

I don't fault them.

What use is a map when the world is labyrinthine?

What use is direction when there are exits at every turn?

(Interlude)

Does the sky look like it could shatter

at any given moment or is that just me?

If I could uninvent the words "priest" and "prayer," then the dead

could come back from the dead for at least a chance at revenge.

Revenge is more decolonial than justice.

Did you know: A group of NDNs is called "a murder"?

A group of NDNs is called "the most photographed thing

in twenty-first-century Canada"?

A white boyfriend of mine wanted me to be less beholden to the clouds.

I told him we are all at the mercy of the sky, for better or worse.

Part of me thinks he didn't deserve to know

about this mode of attention, this art of description.

But I can't keep secrets. I am addicted

to the high of letting my own words forsake me.

When I was a boy,

my mosum told me a story about the day the sky fell down.

The sky is still falling,

but only NDNs can tell the difference.

I look up, and down comes a parade of half-smiling children.

A ROMANCE OF THE PRESENT

A poem is a room
into which I shove my autobiographical self.
In the dark I am a sign
pirouetting into its signifier and signified.
I am especially NDN when trying to convince
someone else I am lovable.
Drunk on hope,
which is the most NDN of all NDN feelings,
I make out with my imaginary NDN lover
in the ashes of every Canadian pastoral poem ever written.
When his slurred words explode inside me,
the past rushes out.
My hobbies include:
not dying,
obsessively apologizing to the moon for all that she has to witness,
and slow dancing to the tune of "Heaven" by Bryan Adams with men
who refuse to give in to the life-changing magic of vulnerability.
Let's call the future heaven
and be done with a romance of the present.
The present was a mistake.
The possibility of anything else is a call to arms.

Listen for the soundscape of the netherworld
that is *the* world!
The quiet begets slow death of all kinds.
We need to train our ears
to hear the chime of historical contingency.
To toe the edge of the unthinkable
is to rend the quiet.
There is an art to forgetting
what the night plays house to.
By now, it must be
something of an NDN tradition.
Still, a book, which coaxes confession,
seems too flimsy for all this longing.
(Oh shit, did I just break the fourth wall or whatever?)

I DOUCHE WHILE KESHA'S "PRAYING" PLAYS FROM MY IPHONE ON REPEAT

I DOUCHE WHILE KESHA'S "PRAYING" PLAYS FROM MY IPHONE ON REPEAT AND SUDDENLY ANAL FLUIDS DEMAND MY SOCIOLOGICAL ATTENTION / PICTURE THIS: TWO BROTHERS, ONE FINDS IN BOOZE WHAT THE OTHER FINDS IN THE BODIES OF WHITE MEN / REFUSE TO CONCEPTUALIZE THE CONSEQUENCES OF THESE CRAVINGS AS ANYTHING BUT EQUALLY DANGEROUS / I AM NO BETTER THAN HE WHO EATS TOO MUCH OF THE SUNSET / IN FACT ALL I DO IS GNAW AND GNAW AT THE SUN UNTIL MY LIPS ARE SO CRACKED I CAN BUT SPEAK THE WORLD WRONG / NOWADAYS WHEN I AM ASKED IF I AM HUNGRY FERAL WORDS DROP FROM MY MOUTH SUCH AS *IS MARK RUFFALO HOTTER BECAUSE HE CARES ABOUT NDNS??? AND NDNS LIKE YOU ARE ALWAYS UNCUT!!!* / BUT MY VOICE STAYS THE SAME SO EVENTUALLY I TOO MISTAKE THE "NOT-I" FOR THE "I" AND NO ONE WARNS YOU ABOUT THE THORNY EDGES OF THE NOT-I BECAUSE NO ONE WANTS TO TALK ABOUT INVOLUNTARY EXILE / NO ONE WANTS TO BECOME TRAPPED IN THE CIRCUITRY OF UNBECOMING WHICH IS PERPETUAL BECAUSE MEMORY CANNIBALIZES ITSELF IN EVEN THE QUEEREST OF BEDROOMS / IF I HAD CATCHPHRASES THEY WOULD BE: *DOES THIS FORESKIN MAKE ME LOOK NDN???* AND *I AM A MOURNER SO PLEASE TELL ME IF I HAVE MOURNING BREATH ACTUALLY YOU KNOW WHAT I THINK I WOULD STILL KISS*

YOU IF YOU HAD MOURNING BREATH I'M SUPER-ACCOMMODATING LIKE THAT!!! / I DON'T WANT TO ADMIT I AM RULED BY ANXIETY SO I WILL OPT FOR THE CLUNKIER "NOSTALGIA FOR THE FUTURE" / I THINK THE PRIME MINISTER IS GASLIGHTING ME / I THINK I AM GASLIGHTING MYSELF / MY MAN HAS ALREADY TORN OFF HIS WOLF'S MASK TO REVEAL A RADIOACTIVE WOLF BENEATH IN ANOTHER DIMENSION / I INSTALL THE SPACE BETWEEN THAT WORLD AND OURS WITH FLAMMABLE MEANING / I MAKE A WILDFIRE OUT OF IT / I TRIP OVER MY OWN TWO FEET TRYING TO RUN FROM IT / LOVE TAUGHT ME HOW TO STARE WITHOUT LOOKING / I DON'T BLINK FOR HOURS / I START TO SMELL LIKE DUST / I DISAGGREGATE INTO A BOX OF OLD KEEPSAKES / WHAT'S MORE A THEORY OF SEXUAL NORMATIVITY IS A SPRING DRESS I WEAR IN THE DEAD OF WINTER / THE LIGHT BULBS START TO GOSSIP ABOUT MY DESPERATE ASS AND YET I CAN'T BRING MYSELF TO STOP EAVESDROPPING / I JOKE THAT I HAVE BEEN SO SLUTTY I AM NO LONGER ATTRACTED TO MEN / IN REALITY I DON'T KNOW HOW TO BE ANYTHING BUT A WIND-UP BOY / WHAT I WANT FROM LOVE IS WHAT I WANT FROM REVOLUTION / MY MAN AND I FUCK WHEN WE RUN OUT OF THINGS TO SAY BECAUSE OUR MOUTHS ARE STILL MOUTHS / WE FUCK IN A HURRY WHEN HISTORY LEAVES THE APARTMENT TO SMOKE A CIGARETTE / WE FUCK SO AS TO SET THE COUNTRY ON FIRE BEFORE IT DOES ME / AFTER ALL THEY SAY ONLY THE GOOD DIE YOUNG / OR WAS IT THE NDNS???

LEONARDO DICAPRIO

My ex-boyfriend got measurably more attractive
and all I got was a dad bod.
Leonardo DiCaprio has a dad bod,
and for whatever reason this is reassuring to me.
Leonardo DiCaprio finally won an Oscar
for his lead role in *The Revenant*.
Leonardo DiCaprio was almost killed by a bear
in said movie. But alas, he wasn't.
I have yet to see *The Revenant*,
but only because there ain't nothing special
about a settler who defies death
while NDNs drop like flies around him.
Case in point: the Wikipedia page
for *The Revenant* is organized into ten sections,
one of which is Plot, the first line of which reads:
"In late 1823, Hugh Glass guides Andrew Henry's
trappers through unorganized territory."
Regardless of what Leonardo DiCaprio had to say at the Oscars
about NDN resistance and climate change,
white people see what they want.
They feast on what's before them.
Had this been a movie made by NDNs,
that bear would have killed

Leonardo DiCaprio in the first ten minutes
and for the next two hours and twenty-six minutes
(because this movie runs two hours and thirty-six minutes)
there would have been no footage,
just the sounds of NDNs
organizing territory.
Whatever the fuck that means!

DUPLEX (THE FUTURE'S A FIST)

The future's a fist; plants me in a bed.
A brief history of flesh starts with a knife.

      History starts into my brief flesh, a knife.
      In my mouth is a chain of white flags.

In the mouths of my white lovers, there are chains.
Is there a heaven for mother tongues?

      Is "heaven" on the tip of my mother's tongue?
      When love turned up, it was a rotten fruit.

When love turned up, my heart was a rotten fruit.
If I die before this country does, don't cry.

      Don't cry before this country does. If I die,
      Blame the postponed mourning, the eye's forest.

The I's a forest, where it's always morning.
The future's a bed of dawn I plant fists in.

CANADIAN HORROR STORY

1.

Tina Fontaine's body was retrieved from the Red River on August 17, 2014, nine days after she was last seen at a hotel in downtown Winnipeg. The Red River is an eight-hundred-and-eighty-five kilometre body of water that meanders through major North American cities such as Fargo, Grand Forks, and Winnipeg. A toxicologist reported that the river, an unknowing accomplice, had washed away the DNA from the duvet in which Tina had been wrapped sometime on August 8. The molecular entities that bore the key to a guilty verdict likely tumbled about the Red River during the criminal investigation. In colder water, the decomposition of DNA is, however, slowed down, so it is also possible that remnants of that violence are still there, in a spectral form, blended into the ecosystem of a river already teeming with NDN history. What happened isn't nowhere; it wasn't disappeared. Who listened to the river? Who didn't?

2.

There is a holy place filled with NDN girls, hair wet with utopia, who were caught between girlhood and a TV death. No, it isn't heaven. The hunted know of greener grasses.

3.

I would unwrite everything to make forever out of August 7, 2014.

4.

It is February 9, 2018. Gerald Stanley is acquitted by an all-white jury in the murder of Colten Boushie, a ceremonial firekeeper from the Red Pheasant First Nation. I am sitting outside my apartment complex, immobilized — centuries of settler rage pooling inside me. The rage pools and pools until a single stone could send a ripple through me, as though I were a puddle. Colten was just a year older than me when he was assailed by a body snatcher, the likes of which lurk everywhere in the prairies. The world is a wound, so I am older than him now. I want clocks to still. I want to impose some sort of justice before any of us are subject to the biological wrath of time. It feels unethical to age.

5.

If I die prematurely, forget burial,
                    just drop my body
                              on the steps
                                   of the Supreme Court
                                        of Canada.

6.

An entire citizenry is implicated. I have just one question left: How does it feel to live in an asylum you built bone by sooty bone? How permanent you made us! Your asylum, outside redemption, outside atonement — I bet it is cold there.

7.

PSA: You can wish to be unslanted by a past you want dead too, but that would make you a terrible person.

8.

How alchemical the white eye is! 1) Sat in a medical office, twenty-four hours without a shower, sweating with tonsillitis: I am data to be mined and nothing else. *I will help you with two things and that's it,* a doctor barks without making eye contact, my body a statue of unfreedom from which one turns away. 2) It is six in the morning and I tiptoe, bowled over with discomfort, into an emergency room, my body protesting movement and calm at once. Two white men are smoothly moved from triage to the doctor's care. I am, however, approached by two security guards — bloated with power (power, however mundane, is never minuscule), comporting themselves as though they were double their actual size. They ask me to sit still in the chair, otherwise I risk forcible removal at their hands. Shortly thereafter, I am pulled aside so a doctor can determine whether or not I am lying about my pain. First Nations people who live in Alberta are expected to die at least a dozen years before other residents of the province. Expecting to die is a manifestation of social death. Do you know how much of the blowback of history an NDN has to caress late at night? It is a wounded and wounding companion! Some nights, it hogs the blankets. Others, it curls up at the foot of the bed. Always, it bares its fangs.

9.

I am counting the ways in which the flesh of NDNs is emptied of ethical substance — towards another mode of enumeration.

10.

What is an NDN if not the ceiling of a country's political imagination?

REGARDING DEATH, I TURN TO THE PHOTON

The largest mass hanging in Canadian history — at Battleford,
Saskatchewan, in 1885, where eight Indigenous men were hanged
for their participation in the North-West Rebellion. Indigenous
children from the nearby Industrial School were forced to watch.
    — Aimée Craft

Regarding death, I turn to the photon:
how, when caught in a line of sight,
it goes on to fragment inside an ordinary face.
There are words to describe what this makes of us,
but I won't go there. Not today.
Not when cumulus clouds
are evaporating at sixty-minute intervals.
Everything is atomizing everywhere all the time,
and yet the average eyeball is just twenty-four millimetres wide.
To build the Cree word for bloodshed, you need the modifier *mistahi*,
which designates quantity — much, a great deal, a lot.
On the other hand, the English word human
originates from *humanus*, a Latin word meaning humane, kind, gentle.
Of course we have come to know ourselves
by what we aren't, much like the modern zoo animal that,
driven mad by boredom, presses the cage into its wanting mouth.
One need but crane up at the night sky

to be reminded of our funereal disposition.
How fitting that we coax the celestially departed into the graveyards of us!
The plot twist is that we too are like stars: even after death
the body briefly emits photons, invisible to the naked eye.
Think, then, of the hanged men, who moved,
if only for a fraction of a second, as light
through those war-torn children,
simultaneously making a brutish violence more brutish
and proving colonial power can't wholly seize the NDN body.
There is so much to be won and lost
in the long tradition of Canadian autopsy!

CANADIAN SONNET

History is a song, a cruel anthem
my nameless lovers mouth all the words of.
Confession: I rarely survive the night
in the biome of a man's longing. What
has been lost doesn't ask to be unlost.
Love's work is always slow, painstaking. We're
allowed forgetfulness. Men I fuck don't
believe people can rust. I'm not unique.
Memory? Pardon the melodrama
— it's raining again in the apartment.
Funny how suddenly the body turns
into a Canadian monument!
I'd rather be a bird. Do birds grow sick
of the exploding sky? Would NDNs?

NDN HOMO SONNET

An NDN is the ellipsis of a nation.
Even in God's palm, a homo is a yearning
the size of a world. Is an invisible spectacle
a paradox? Is a good melancholia? Mathematically
speaking, an NDN homo is a metaphysical conundrum.
Put differently, I am a mother before all else.
Maggie Nelson speculates that a mother
is "the archetypal Levinasian subject,"
which is to say my lover is two fingers pulling
apart the mouth of a planet. He is a dancer.

To him, my living is the sound of an emptying.
When I die, it will still be autumn in my body.
I trust he will dust my shadow off so as to watch it tangle
in dusk's wild mane. I was a windswept "I" from the start.

II.

Fawcett, AB

WRITE AGAINST THE UNWRITABILITY OF GRIEF TO WRITE AGAINST THE UNWRITABILITY OF GRIEF
WRITE AGAINST THE UNWRITABILITY OF GRIEF TO WRITE AGAINST THE UNWRITABILITY OF GRIEF
WRITE AGAINST THE UNWRITABILITY OF GRIEF TO WRITE AGAINST THE UNWRITABILITY OF GRIEF
WRITE AGAINST THE UNWRITABILITY OF GRIEF TO WRITE AGAINST THE UNWRITABILITY OF GRIEF
WRITE AGAINST THE UNWRITABILITY OF GRIEF TO WRITE AGAINST THE UNWRITABILITY OF GRIEF
WRITE AGAINST THE UNWRITABILITY OF GRIEF TO WRITE AGAINST THE UNWRITABILITY OF GRIEF

TREATY 8

THE LIMITS

OF

REPRESENTING

INDIAN SUBJECTS

AND TO ARRANGE THEM

WILL THEM AND

OTHER SUBJECTS

TO

RELEASE, SURRENDER
AND YIELD UP

TO THE

LIMITS   IS TO SAY: THE SOURCE
OF   THE RED

INTERSECTS

IN THE

MOUTH OF   A

STRAIGHT LINE   THENCE

THE

BOUNDARY OF

THE PLACE OF

THE

WHEREVER

TO HOLD

THE

DESCRIBED, SUBJECT TO   A

TIME   OF

DESIRE TO

EXCEED ONE S

NUMBER TO RESIDE

IN

SEVERALTY

TO BE A PROVISO

TO BE MADE IN THE

APART

AND OPEN

FOR

THE BOUNDS OF

THE

OTHERWISE

THE INDIANS

APPROPRIATED ████████████████████████████

██

██

██

██

██

THE ▊ PAST ████

TO MAKE

EACH ▊▊ A PRESENT ████████████

OF

WHATEVER AGE ████████████ THE TIME

AND PLACE OF ████████████████████

██████████████████████████████████

A ████ FLAG, AND ████████████

████████████████████████████████████

OF ████████████████████

████████████████ CHILDREN ████

████████████████████████████████████

████████████████████████████████████

THE ████

████████████████████████████████████

████████████████████████████████████

SIGNIFIED ████████████████████

████████████████████████████████████

FORKS

THE
LOCALITY

A   REAPER

GIVEN   ALL   THE
ENCOURAGEMENT
TO CONTINUE HUNTING

ON
BEHALF   OF   THE

LAW;   THE

INDIANS

CEDE

JUNE

IN WITNESS

IN WITNESS

WITNESS

THE

TERMS   UNTO WHICH

THE

HANDS

ADHERE TO

THE

RIVER

OF JULY

AND ███ THE ██████ LAKE ███

██████████████████ OF ████

███████████████████████████

███████████████████████████

███████████████████████████

███████████████████████████

███████████████████████████

██████████ A ███ COUNTRY ███

███████████████████████████

██████ HAVING HAD █████ TO ███

███████████████████████████

███████████████████████████

███████████████████████████

CONSIDER ██████████████████

███████████████████████████

███████████████████████████

███████████████████████████

███████████████████████████

███████████████████████████

███████████████████████████

THE CESSION MADE BY THE SAID

THE INDIANS

OF THE

PRESENT

HONOUR

THE TERMS

OF THE UN

WRITTEN.

ARS POETICA

In an essay called "Is There Any Poetic Writing?," Roland Barthes
argues that words do not merely "reproduce the depth and singularity
of an individual experience." For him, "they are spread out to form a
surface."

I wrote a poem to resemble a forest floor teeming with decaying vegetation.
A struggling thing isn't a struggling thing
if everything else is in a state of rot.
Nothing can be turned inside out if "inside" and "out"
are free-floating concepts in a world without direction.
No one wants to be a free-floating concept
unless emptiness is a harrowing feat.

*

Warsan Shire: "You can't make homes out of human beings."
I've seen homesick insomniacs, uninterested in rest,
engineer bedrooms out of the loose skin of the poet.
I too have laid myself flat on the sullied mattress of a poem,
if only to roll off the edge
of a line break.

*

A poem is a funhouse with warped mirrors.
From it, one gleans
a distorted image of oneself.
A poem, however, isn't a mirror.
A mirror wants nothing for itself.
A poem, a surface
to boomerang a future history, a future past.

FLESH*

To locate a living

concept

Identity   hear

dies hard   Indian people

and   speak.

the world is not so simple   *

not always realistic.   Historians of sexuality

Worldviews   kill each other

are   bluntly

women   forcefully

who lived their whole life   in this field

in archives   of

examined and reexamined.   beautiful boys.

What is now needed is more. Songs, poems, plays, and

no.   literature

*   ethnographies of

---

* Here is an erasure poem composed of words and phrases that follow sequentially in the first five chapters of Walter L. Williams's infamous anthropological account of non-normative gender and sexuality in Indigenous communities, *The Spirit and the Flesh* (1986). At the end of chapter five, I stopped because I felt a story had been adequately told. Williams painted a picture of queer and trans NDN life as deeply binary; his view was, of course, slanted by a fetishistic curiosity emptied of ethical investment in the studied. "Flesh" is my attempt at offering up a counterhistory via a kind of linguistic archaeology, to excavate the incendiary voices of queer, trans, and two-spirit ancestors whose language was at once a hyperobject and unknowable in the world of ethnographic inquiry. I had two rules: 1) the words and phrases had to adhere to the book's chronology, and 2) each word or phrase had to initiate a new line break in the hopes that the minimalist structure and the vast blankness of the page might gesture to the kinds of language drowned out at a time when hard-fought ideas were being cemented in regard to their survivability, and therefore ours.

doubt
written ·
ashamed of
holiness.

*

Condemned
for acting like women
the
women
created
two worlds that they lived in
bleak and unhappy
escaped
the first
a
new
women's work
to continue living
in
translation.
Desires of the heart
like
women's clothing
only a pile of stones

a
dress
speaking.

*

The boy
a circle
to crowd
the boy
bathed
in childhood
set fire to
the boy
a
symbolic gesture
the
boy
was
reflexes
not
free will.
Once a person
is
named
a man

he
is
not
light
but
circumlocution
a burning
a
worried
hunger
a
total darkness
a boy
is
a wolf
a promise of good hunting.

*

Indians
rebelled against
Being
male speech
could not
force
a way out

from
the
human
this
alien
spirituality.

*

Understanding
the beginning of the nineteenth
century
as
feelings
so great
made them
an atmosphere
of disaster:
the sick
song
everyone sang
the wings
near our faces
the room
for burial
every

tree
the branches above our heads
their
dance.
You can
kill me
in public
they expect it
too
Indian
so
faggot
you always find at least one
struck by lightning
the weather
a pair of
h
a
n
d
s.
*
The
dying day
fit into

a child
he seems to resemble
a
house
no one tries to
live
in.
Some anthropologists
face pain and death
through
warfare
with burning sticks
they
impose on a child
gender
a small boy
to become a
brutal
little world.
*
Female talk
a tongue
against
America
that

drunk

summer

we

are

subjected to.

*

What

glory

to live

in

shame

like

arrows

in

a

wound.

MELANCHOLY'S FORMS

In Freud's wake, it is something of an axiom that melancholy occurs outside the rhythms of everyday life. For Freud, melancholy is a response to loss that compels one to feast on the dead. Devoured, the lost object is incorporated into the one who mourns, kept in the world as a cheapened abstraction. Unable to relinquish the object from her sense of self, she who grieves out loud floats above the world of the lively and uncomplicatedly emotive. A negation of a negation, the lost object becomes ghoulish, much like the necromancer in which it is made to reside. Under the watch of the psychoanalyst, the melancholic becomes an automaton with which he participates in the cruel art of categorization.

In her seminal text *Gender Trouble: Feminism and the Subversion of Identity*, Judith Butler makes the case that gender identification is a melancholic process in a culture of compulsory heterosexuality. By way of skilled psychoanalytic judgements, Butler posits that one is made to disavow the "same-sexed object" as a site of desire and instead to incorporate it as a part of an affectively endowed becoming-subject. Banished to the netherworld of the unreal, "homosexual love," to use Butler's language, is fixed to the status of "never was." This, Butler says in her essay, "Melancholy Gender — Refused Identification," published twenty years after *Gender Trouble*, is what partly conditioned the ungrievability of those lost to the AIDS epidemic, losses accelerated by governmental neglect, the trapdoors of signification, and the neoliberal spoils of forward thinking. In the land of the lost, queerness is ephemera and ephemera is "trace, the remains, the things that are left, hanging in the air like a rumor" (José Esteban Muñoz). Queerness: at once what never was and what is still to come.

The settler arrives at the shores of identity too via the magic trick of melancholia. Away from lands governed in his name, the settler pines after a new mode of indigenization. Faced with the ethical dilemma of NDN presence, the settler employs ruses of recognition to make the NDN governable, to rid NDN nations of their practices of territoriality. In its grisliest form, settler melancholy drives many to slaughter. In both cases, the NDN is annihilated, made into a loss that the settler absorbs, that enlivens a new sovereign "I." This might partly explain why the unending production of NDN suffering has skirted the labour of compassion. Left to die in the ditch of history, the NDN lays bare a form of pain unhearable in the theatres of liberal redress.

Melancholy:
the hospice care of memory.

Spilled, unbound, remote, unsafe, melancholy swells in the badlands of modernity. There, it rejigs words so as to expose that which is always in excess of what we utter, a chorus of linguistic surplus. This is less about an anthropology from below than about a desire to beget the finality of desire, to roam instead through the underground of semiotics. We speak polyphonically, against the white noise of the present, its fable of the world, to become a public enemy to the poets. We tiptoe into the field of vision of the sky, to make ourselves judicable. Under siege in the barracks of the prairies, we concoct our own social experiment, one without end, an unmoneyed one, alive and indeterminate, but always rebellious. Tomorrow, we surrender to the frenzy of the surround of the surround.

In the back alley of the world, melancholy is a utopian feeling. The back alley is both a metaphor and a material condition. It is a deformity of the law; there, the codes of public life are upended and everything and nothing is criminal. In an archipelago of exile like ours, there are crowds everywhere. For a second or two, everyone has but one skin, wired to the feeling of being on the run. It isn't that we are escaping life, but that we were stranded by it. An ocean flooded the basement of us. Always, in and out are durational concepts, and as such they fail to provide any sense of place. Indeed, the sole orientation one can have is that of vertigo. GPS is a relic of a bygone era. Flags are always at half-mast, which is to say ours is a no man's land. Tonight, we make a country out of one another.

HYPOTHESES

A poem in which my anxiety morphs into a folding chair that doesn't open — furniture against the teleology of the commodity.

A poem in which I reach into my throat with a wire hanger to fish out my manhood, also a wire hanger.

A poem in which I howl into the lockjawed night and it radicalizes absent fathers everywhere.

A poem in which whiteness is abolished, so it is also a poem in which we kick our shoes off for the first time.

A poem in which I don't survive the affective wrath of bad art made for the anti-care theologians.

A poem in which a museum is crowded by a murmuration of cops acquitted of murder; they march as one into a history of extinction.

A poem in which a government of NDN women legislates away the non-event of reconciliation.

A poem in which yesterday never comes; a poem in which we love at the speed of utopia, leaving our shipwrecked country no time to begin anew.

DESIRE MADE WASTE OUT OF TIME

Feminist theorist Rosi Braidotti announces that we are in "post-AIDS days" where "queer mutants seem to enjoy special favor" / desire made waste out of time but it was never a waste of time / there are dead ends that open up onto dead ends / what is a mutant to a mutant but arrogated blame / if we are all material-semiotic, what is a mutant but material-semiotic-poetic / in a world fashioned by shame, the AIDS epidemic haunts queer poetry / listen: to be haunted isn't merely a psychologically fraught response to a past one has irrevocably and impossibly lost / haunting is a theory of ethics that posits one's non-sovereignty vis-à-vis the exteriority of the self / death by misrecognition is a problem for ethics, for example / haunting, then, is a corrective to the heteronormative fetish of the individual / it is thus not my name I would rescue from a burning building / a name, in the end, is little more than an incitement to incalculable carnage.

Driftpile Cree Nation

RED UTOPIA

"Is it possible to write about making things without also provoking desire for them?" So goes Anne Boyer in *Garments Against Women*. Note to self: write a poem about poems about sex. Make a clever observation about how signification was what fished you out of the dirty puddle of undesirability. Seen through the windows of the digital, I was an abstraction. I represented everything; who doesn't want to fuck everything? A man I was dating at the time would sleep with one me (an animal-monster) and slow dance to the sound of nothing with another me (a symbol-lie) (after Boyer). We bathed in the acoustics of desire, in the density of a social music that wasn't the noise of the extraordinary. It went on like this for a few months: I was a metaphor he felt stomached by. Tripped up on the ecstasy of fragility, we nested into a debt we knew we couldn't shoulder on our own. No one could see what was there, so what was there was ours. Maybe my propensity for utopian thinking is positively correlated with the agony of being in a world poisonous for those who knowingly reside in the shadows of the not-yet. Maybe it is a coping mechanism. So what?

Find me cruising in the back alleys of Google Earth. "I was busy thinking 'bout boys / boys, boys / I was busy dreaming 'bout boys / boys, boys" (Charli XCX). Selfishly, I want a world where no one has abs. I want a world where there are no ghosts in the machine of relationality. Intimacy will not be a trap door. A trap door will not be a refuge. A refuge will not be whatever dulls the feeling of aliveness. Aliveness will not be hope against all odds.

In the future, my body will not be an anthropological given. It will know nothing of ethnography, nor the ruses of interpellation. I will outgrow it the night I let the cat out of the bag. By "it" I mean a siphon for that which is disappeared when we designate anything "the private." By "cat" I mean the purr of subjectification. By "out of the bag" I mean to say that I will hurl words into the world with such intensity I could risk reifying a pornography of the dead. No, not necrophilia. Rather, something like scopophilia. Which is to say there is pleasure to be absorbed from the racialized spectacle of contortion that is confessional poetry. Under which conditions is a body simply raw material for the industries of analysis? I digress. Soon, there will be theoreticians everywhere but the university, so there will be no need for the cannibalism of the social sciences.

I want to write a book about queer indigeneity entitled *Loneliness as a Way of Life*. Alas, someone has already written a book with that title, so maybe I would call it *It Is Lonely to Be Alive*. It would enflesh my suspicion that if indigeneity = ante-ontology and queerness = anti-subjectivity, then queer indigeneity agitates ideation. That we make philosophy into a falsity incompatible with explanation evinces we are inhabitants of a lopsided place we might call the somewhere/time, which is ruled by the felt knowledge that the otherworldly is a core facet of NDN life. In the somewhere/time, in the land of the un-, optimism is neither cruel nor does it get swallowed up in an emotional economy of scarcity. Loneliness, the affective state of being in a world one doesn't want, makes utopia a thinkable concept. If loneliness is a kind of dysphoria with the world, then let's deal a crushing blow to the tyranny of materiality! "Join me down here in nowhere" (Claudia Rankine)! It is lonely to be alive!

What is it to speak of a social poesis of the reserve? In the aftermath of a noxious history that repeats, there is an ever-proliferating body of scholarly writing that describes the particularities of the "bio-necropolitical" (Jasbir Puar) gulag that is the reserve. Life is difficulty made outside the wrath of misery. But, the reserve is also a site of the not not-yet of utopia. Against a teleological rendering of utopia as an end always tantalizingly to come, I understand those on the reserve to be denizens of the world. Already enmeshed in a structure of feeling contra a Canadian sensorium, those of the reserve are synced to a choreography of alternatives, of revolutionary affect. Which means we relish in "the possibility of everything you can't see" (Joy Harjo). When the day ends, so too does Canada.

I look only at the underbelly of the map. Locatable there is that which lives below the threshold of social reality. Rogue, unwatched, paradox enlivens the ontologically dead. Un-. Un-. Un-: a prefix is a portal. The astray is a concept I haven't given up on. In 2015, I argued that the astray is a geography below or beside the everyday. Doomed lovers and historians of the future are its tenants. There, the temporality of love is sped up and thus engenders a modality of intimate life that is feral. The haptics of ferality: convulse, contort, lurch. Everywhere, there are "I"s on me/us. They fall from me/us like mud.

"It is embarrassing to be pornography; it is embarrassing to not be pornography" (Boyer). Am I a traitor to myself (following Maggie Nelson's nod to Deleuze/Parnet in *The Argonauts*)? Am I an "endless, wandering pit of need" (Leanne Betasamosake Simpson) into which anyone could plunge? Do I offer up an "I," however mangled, for the sake of vampiric consumption? The feminist knows this is an old pastime. The NDN knows this is the bloodied scene of an enactment of settler law. The NDN feminist knows this is multitudinous and pervasive, hidden in the low hum of context. How to punctuate an aesthetics of suffering, its visibilization regime, with a counternarrative of NDN possibility? Hypothesis: be negative space.

NOTES FROM THE FIELD

1. Are we in agreement that self-making is seldom politically useful? The political is preceded by the discomfitures of embodiment. Embodiment is a losing game. Yet, here you are.

1. I bet you fantasize about being carried away by a cliché. One moment you are in a sweltering affectsphere with the rest of us; the next you are pounding your fist with the force of a stubborn summer on a lover's chest as though it were a door. And it is. Just like that. Unquestionably.

1. We are in an afterlife of the horrors of the long twentieth century called the supernatural. The border looms as the impending atmosphere of the whole world.

1. Overstimulated, dizzied, I am engrossed by the reverberations of the un-institutional. Yes, that was a reference to Foucault's "Friendship as a Way of Life." I am always referencing Foucault's "Friendship as a Way of Life." I oscillate between Grindr and an essay about Toronto's Grindr serial killer. This is a reference to Foucault. My boyfriend farts and I politely ignore it. Later, I say: *You know, it's okay for you to fart near me. As long as it isn't, like, horribly smelly!* This too is a reference to Foucault.

1. Top me, but ontologically.

1. I am a grammarian of a decomposing language. I dream in English and wake up underwater.

1. A man + arrows shot into the earth = a nation. Centuries later, a girl plucks the fletching the way she would the heads of dandelions. Something innate inside her rebels against form. Slowly, the rain melts her cardboard-cutout body.

1. Another sticky dawn. The rez opens its eyes. The past hiccups. Dogs holler back. In a bed, someone who is loved is found dead (from cancer or heart disease or mercury poisoning, which are history by other names). The religiously minded suspect God is a thief who works under the cover of night, that even he keeps watch of the rez, which must look like a regular accident from so high up. Death, codified in this way, is an aesthetic experience for which no one is answerable. Others, however, believe blame is a hungry beast, that its heartbeat is theirs. The rez opens its mouth. Screams.

1. Canada is a glass wall I bash my teeth into.

1. Remember: one person's unlivable life is another's plagiarized guilt.

FRAGMENTS ENDING WITH A REQUIEM

Let us undertake an ethnomusicology of tears. I am after the frequency of NDN grievability. My hunch is that the pitch interrogates itself, like a hymn. What I know: a primal shout is a counteranthropological event, though unsustainable as a performance of politics. Does futurity have a sound? Does agelessness? What is a noiseless poetry? Utopia? When I fell in love, sound devoured itself—this is the hospitality of silence. Before Canada, there was an unfillable quiet. An ancestral chant not yet heard anew.

*

Indigeneity is to futurity as desire is to historical revisionism.

*

Smudge me with the lights out.

*

My kokum is the Minister of Utopia is NDN AF.

*

The poem is a container for a beauty on the run from terror. Step inside. We are traffic-jammed with joy here.

*

Can one be against data and still be for kinship?

*

In the end, it wasn't intelligibility we were after.

*

I plant my head in the earth and then I am a tree — a metaphysical tree that bears neither fruit nor sap, but limbs.

*

I hang from the ceiling with my cruel nostalgia. My cruel nostalgia shimmers.

*

The countrymen took our conviviality to be an accusation. So be it!

*

Art is emotional. Emotion is artful. The purpose of art and emotion for the NDN is to escape the sociolinguistic prison of a white vernacular. My books are emotional and artful only insofar as they are criminal.

*

My tongue is a parking garage; men arrived with deflated tires.

*

What distinguishes denotation from detonation, after all, is human invention. Blood-letting a people with the alphabet is a gutting just the same.

*

One can't rule out the possibility of violence as a response to violence. Indeed, comprehension is kick-started by a seizure of visual information. I ask questions that frustrate answerability. This is a form of violence. I pit language against itself and want nothing clean to come of it. This too is a form of violence.

*

All this talk of how poetry brings us closer to language, but what if it's already left? Found a gentler species? Warmer mouths?

I BELIEVE I EXIST

There are many ways to consume other people. — Gwen Benaway

Eradicate a concept, for example.
Without hope, I am a thick fog, stained by what I gobble up
— something to weather.
Under a starved light, I am a sticky dance floor
on which a poem has been written.
On Saturday nights,
I get stickier and stickier until I am not a dance floor anymore.
Someone death drops.
YAAAAAAAAAAS!
Someone drops dead,
but he isn't white so no one is there to see it.
Except everyone is there to see it,
they are just too busy thinking about how much
they have changed for the better to open their fucking eyes.
I am a drag queen named Commodity Fetishism.
I perform to Rihanna's "Bitch Better Have My Money,"
except by "money" I mean "body."
I am an abstraction of an abstraction of an abstraction and so on.
I am a glass half-shattered.
What is a ghost to a ghost but photocopied pity?
Sometimes I want the language of a non-place,

but no language is placeless.
Prove to me that he who despises the world
isn't also transfixed by it.
I believe I exist.
To live, one can be neither
more nor less hungry than that.
I believe I existed.
One can't be left hungrier than that.

A men's bathroom stall in West Edmonton Mall, AB.

NOTES

The epigraphs are from Ocean Vuong's *On Earth We're Briefly Gorgeous* (2019) and Anne Carson's *Autobiography of Red* (1998).

"The Terrible Beauty of the Reserve" is after Saidiya Hartman's "The Terrible Beauty of the Slum" (2017).

In "A Lover's Discourse," "A boy in love with a boy . . ." is indebted to Ocean Vuong's phraseology of "a body sleeping / beside a boy / must make a field / full of ticking" in *Night Sky with Exit Wounds* (2016).

In "The Wall Clock Caught Fire from Neglect," the image of an "open-air church" comes to me from Alice Oswald's *Memorial* (2011): "you might rip the roof off a church in order to remember what you're worshipping."

"At the Mercy of the Sky" has lines that draw inspiration from Danez Smith's long poem "summer, somewhere"; in particular, the lines "there is no language / for *officer* or *law*" and "no need for geography. / now, that we're safe everywhere."

In "I Douche while Kesha's 'Praying' Plays from My iPhone on Repeat," "HE WHO EATS TOO MUCH OF THE SUNSET" is recycled from my poem "Rez Sisters II" in *This Wound is a World*. "STARE WITHOUT LOOKING" is an inversion of Tanya Lukin Linklater's "look without staring." "NOSTALGIA FOR THE FUTURE" is also the name of a film by Avijit Mukul Kishore and Rohan Shivkumar (2017) and a book by Charles Piot (2010).

Much gratitude to Jericho Brown for inventing the form of the duplex, which is a fusion of the ghazal, the sonnet, and the blues, as seen partially modified in "Duplex (The Future's a Fist)."

In "Canadian Horror Story," the analysis in number one bears an analytical inheritance from Christina Sharpe's discussion of "residence time" in *In the Wake: On Blackness and Being* (2016); "forget burial..." is a remixing of a well-known motto of late twentieth-century AIDS activists: "If I die of AIDS, forget burial, just drop my body on the steps of the FDA."

"Regarding Death, I Turn to the Photon" also appears in the edition of *This Wound is a World* published in the U.S. by the University of Minnesota Press.

In "NDN Homo Sonnet," the Maggie Nelson reference is from a lecture archived on YouTube as "Maggie Nelson Lecture" by PNCA Live Video.

In "I Believe I Exist," "Prove to me that he who despises the world / isn't also transfixed by it" is in conversation with Anne Boyer's "And there was, I thought, a reasonably justifiable distinction between she was who captivated by the imagination and she who was captivated by the world" in *Garments Against Women* (2015).

Works referenced in the poems include: Anne Boyer's *Garments Against Women* (2015), Claudia Rankine's *Citizen: An American Lyric* (2014), Judith Butler's *Gender Trouble: Feminism and the Subversion of Identity* (1990) and her essay "Melancholy Gender — Refused Identification" (2009), Jasbir Puar's *Terrorist Assemblages: Homonationalism in Queer Times* (2007), Joy Harjo's *Secrets from the Center of the World* (1990), Leanne Betasamosake Simpson's *This Accident of Being Lost*

(2017), Maggie Nelson's *The Argonauts* (2015), Rosi Braidotti's *The Post-human* (2013), José Esteban Muñoz's *Cruising Utopia: The Then and There of Queer Futurity* (2009), Roland Barthes's essay "Is There Any Poetic Writing?" (1953), Warsan Shire's poem "For Women Who Are 'Difficult' to Love," and Gwen Benaway's essay "Holy Wild" (2017).

ACKNOWLEDGEMENTS

Earlier versions of poems printed herein were published in or by the following: *The Walrus*, the Academy of American Poets, *Vallum Magazine*, *C Magazine*, *The Rumpus*, *The Humber Literary Review*, *Colorado Review*, PRISM international, *Prairie Fire/CV2*, *Eighteen Bridges*, and *Brick*. "Melancholy's Forms" appeared in a publication edited by Vanessa Kwan and Kimberly Phillips as part of an exhibition called *Unwilling: Exercises in Melancholy* out of Haverford College. A version of "I Douche while Kesha's 'Praying' Plays from My iPhone on Repeat" was published in Elissa Washuta and Theresa Warburton's *Shapes of Native Nonfiction* (2019). Much gratitude to the editors who marshalled the poems into the world with care.

To each audience that received these poems in their infancies, thank you for your attention and openness!

Brittany and Courtney, your sorority and deep love buoy me!

Kevin Connolly's sharp editorial eye made this book stronger at the levels of craft, structure, and form. Thank you! Love to everyone at House of Anansi Press for welcoming this quirky book and me into your ranks!

I owe an immense debt to my powerhouse agent, Stephanie Sinclair, who took me on as a client before I was cool, haha. Your rigour, belief, and vision continue to astound me!

A final expression of gratitude for the NDN writers/artists with whom I've had the luck of being in orbit — now is the time to make a world in the image of our radical art!

BILLY-RAY BELCOURT is from the Driftpile Cree Nation and lives on the Internet. His debut book of poems, *This Wound is a World,* won the 2018 Griffin Poetry Prize and the 2018 Robert Kroetsch City of Edmonton Book Prize, and was named the Most Significant Book of Poetry in English by an Emerging Indigenous Writer at the 2018 Indigenous Voices Awards. It was also a finalist for the Governor General's Literary Award, the Gerald Lampert Memorial Award, and the Raymond Souster Award. It was named by CBC Books as the best Canadian poetry collection of the year. His book *A History of My Brief Body* was a #1 national bestseller; a *Globe and Mail* Best Book of the Year; and a finalist for the Governor General's Literary Award, the Lambda Literary Award for Gay Memoir/ Biography, and two BC and Yukon Book Prizes. Billy-Ray was a 2018 Pierre Elliott Trudeau Foundation Scholar and earned his Ph.D. in English at the University of Alberta. A 2016 Rhodes Scholar, he holds a master's degree in Women's Studies from Wadham College at the University of Oxford. He is an Assistant Professor in the Creative Writing Program at the University of British Columbia.